ZEN
HAIKU

ZEN
HAIKU

POEMS AND LETTERS
OF NATSUME SŌSEKI

translated and edited by
SŌIKU SHIGEMATSU

Inklings

First edition, 1994

Published by Weatherhill, Inc., 420 Madison Avenue,
15th Floor, New York, NY 10017. Protected by copyright
under terms of the International Copyright Union; all rights
reserved. Except for fair use in book reviews, no part of this
book may be reproduced for any reason by any means,
including any method of photographic reproduction, without
permission of the publisher. Printed in the United States.

Part-title calligraphy by Sōiku Shigematsu.

Library of Congress Cataloging in Publication Data

Natsume, Sōseki, 1867–1916.
  [Poems. English. Selections]
  Zen haiku: poems and letters of Natsume Sōseki / trans-
lated by Sōiku Shigematsu
     p.   cm.
  ISBN 0-8348-0324-0
 1. Natsume, Sōseki, 1867–1916—Translations into
English.
I. Shigematsu, Sōiku, 1943– . II. Natsume, Sōseki
1867–1916. Correspondence. English. Selections. 1994.
III. Title.
PL812.A8A27 1994
895.6'142—dc20
                                           94-28439
                                             CIP

CONTENTS

ACKNOWLEDGMENTS

I would like to extend my deepest gratitude to Professor Dan McLeod, who spent much time assisting me in the early stages of these translations; to Professor Ed Foster, who gave some of my translations (twenty pieces from "Winter") a chance to appear in the *Talisman* (No. 6, Spring 1991); to Inoue Zenjō Rō-Oshō, who gave me information on Sōseki; to Ms. Beverly Ferrel and Ms. Sara Backer for their assistance with English translation, and to Mr. Ray Furse and the others at Weatherhill who joined in the making of this book.

Thanks should also be given to the Museum of Modern Japanese Literature and the Museum of Contemporary Art, Tokyo, for their kind permission to reproduce examples of Sōseki's paintings and calligraphy.

This book stems from the Sōseki research I have been engaged in since my early twenties. Looking back over the past thirty years, I realize I owe much to Akizuki Ryōmin Rōshi for his illuminating viewpoints on Sōseki; to Professor Umehara Takeshi for his stimulating books; and to two late professors, Jugaku Bunshō, who often sent me encouraging letters, and Masutani Fumio, my very first teacher in the true sense of the term. (All names are in the Japanese order, surname first.)

My sincerest gratitude goes to Sōseki himself, because it is he who showed me the best model for a spiritual path between the traditions of East and West, that is, between my twin careers as a professor of English and American literature and as a Zen priest. Now, at fifty, I have finished this book, but Sōseki at this age had finished a lifetime.

Natsume Sōseki (1867–1916)

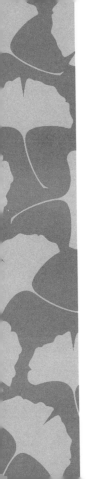

Introduction

Natsume (family name) Sōseki (a personal and pen name) has been one of the most popular and important Japanese writers since the latter half of the nineteenth century, a period that saw a closed, feudal nation transformed into a new Japan open to Western civilization. Sōseki's representative novels are among the most widely read in Japanese literature.

Natsume Kinnosuke (Sōseki's true personal name) was born in 1867 in Tokyo. After an unhappy childhood due to a complex family background, he entered Tokyo University in 1890 to study English literature. Toward the end of 1894 he experienced Zen for the first time when he spent ten days in Zen exercises (*sanzen*) at the Kigen-in temple of the Engakuji complex.

After graduation from the university, he became a junior high school teacher in Matsuyama and in 1896 moved to Kumamoto to teach at a high school.

In 1900, at age thirty-four, Sōseki went to England as a government-sponsored student, but his life in London was not a happy one. He suffered from loneliness and poverty, and a rumor that he had gone mad even reached Japan. One fruitful outcome of this unhappy period, however, was the establishment of his concept of "self-centeredness" (*jiko hon'i*). In January of 1903, he returned to Japan and in April of that year replaced Lafcadio Hearn as a lecturer in English literature at Tokyo University.

Wagahai wa neko de aru (I am a Cat), the first novel of Sōseki's writing career, appeared in 1905. The following year two

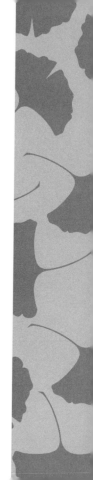

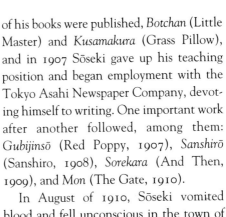

of his books were published, *Botchan* (Little Master) and *Kusamakura* (Grass Pillow), and in 1907 Sōseki gave up his teaching position and began employment with the Tokyo Asahi Newspaper Company, devoting himself to writing. One important work after another followed, among them: *Gubijinsō* (Red Poppy, 1907), *Sanshirō* (Sanshiro, 1908), *Sorekara* (And Then, 1909), and *Mon* (The Gate, 1910).

In August of 1910, Sōseki vomited blood and fell unconscious in the town of Shuzenji due to a severe gastric ulcer. This serious illness led him into a deeper world of the spirit. The next year he refused to accept the honor of a Ph.D. and, fighting both his physical ailment and impending nervous breakdown, he continued to publish successive masterpieces yearly: *Higan sugi made* (Until after the Equinox, 1912),

Kōjin (The Wayfarer, 1913), *Kokoro* (The Heart, 1914), *Michikusa* (Grass on the Wayside, 1915), and his final unfinished novel, *Meian* (Light and Darkness, 1916).

In terms of spiritual development, Sōseki's life may be divided into three periods: the years of dependence upon society and tradition; the years of *jiko hon'i*; and the final years of "following heaven, leaving self" (*sokuten kyoshi*). During his stay in London, Sōseki had confronted modern Western individualism, which regards the individual as a basic indivisible and independent entity. He reflected on his native country, whose citizens neglected their own traditions and looked only abroad for something "civilized." He abhorred their blind allegiance to Western civilization, and thought that Japanese, including himself, needed to develop a spirit of independence.

However, a strong insistence on individuality inevitably provokes competitiveness, and it is but a step from true individualism to selfishness or egotism. Sōseki was certainly keenly aware of this basic weakness of human nature, while still benefiting from other advantageous aspects of Western individualism.

Finally, however, Sōseki sought after something beyond human affairs and ultimately realized the higher spiritual stage of *sokuten kyoshi*. He refers to this idea nowhere in his writings, but talked about it among his circle of acquaintances and admirers, and created a few calligraphic pieces featuring it. His goal of selflessness or egolessness (*muga*) was the crystallization of a keen interest in Zen he had possessed since his younger days.

In addition to being a great novelist, Sōseki was a fine calligrapher, painter, and haiku poet, as well as an excellent composer of Chinese poetry. It is known that he greatly admired the calligraphy of the famous Zen monk Ryōkan (1758–1831), whose works served as a model, and it is also known that in his final years Sōseki treasured friendships with two young Zen monks and exchanged letters with them. Although he usually threw other letters away, after his death his wife found the monk's letters carefully and neatly stored inside his desk. Excerpts from several are included here.

In his haiku and Chinese poems as well, we can see Sōseki's strong attachment to the Zen philosophy and way of life. Careful readers will often find in his works quotations from, or references to, popular and essential Zen sayings from the *Zenrin kushû*, (A Zen Forest, whose abridged

version is included in the Weatherhill
Inklings series).

For this small collection, which appro-
priately appears on the one hundredth
anniversary of his *sanzen* at Enkakuji,
haiku of Sōseki have been chosen that sug-
gest various aspects of Zen—its universali-
ty, individuality, and vitality. Each haiku
has been translated into a three-line free
form verse with as much emphasis on the
Zen viewpoint as possible. In the course of
editing, more than a hundred poems were
omitted that would have required exten-
sive explanation or that are important but
too Japanese in expression. Included with
the haiku are anecdotes about Sōseki,
excerpts from his letters addressed to two
Zen monks, and references to him made by
other important Zen personages, including
Shaku Sōen and D.T. Suzuki.

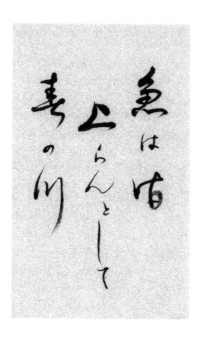

The fish
All struggling upstream:
River in spring.

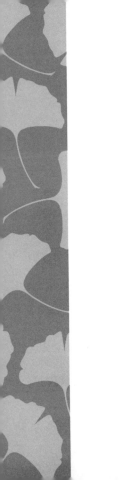

 *Spring*

To Zen monk Kimura Genjō
April 18, 1915

Yesterday I returned home after a month away and enjoyed reading your description of Zen monastery life. I felt much interest in it because it is unfamiliar to me.

Chūhō Oshō's admonition is very good. I have memorized some of Daitō's and Musō's writings, but I can't tell which is which. I remember Chūhō's poem on the importance of birth and death. I'm no Zen scholar, but I have read some Dharma poems and essays (especially those written in Japanese). I regret, however, that I cannot enter the Zen world, remaining as ever a mere layman . . .

To Zen monk Tomizawa Keidō
April 22, 1915

I don't know how many years older I am than you, but I do wish I could live until you become a respected Zen master and I attend your Zen lecture. Should I be dead by that time, please chant a sutra in front of my tomb. Should you arrive in time for my funeral ceremony, please address to my spirit words of guidance into the other world. Although I have no specific religion, I would appreciate a sutra chanted by a noble Zen priest who favors me.

I am heartily grateful to Mr. Kimura, who wrote for me, even in spite of his tight schedule, a long introduction to everyday life at the Zen monastery . . .

Under the plum tree,
Meeting and passing each other,
Exchanging no words.

Head tilted up—
A reed-hatted man's
Flower viewing.

The fish
All struggling upstream:
River in spring.

The rain is over:
South Mountain puffs out
Spring clouds.

One house stands
In the midst of
Spring wind and spring water.

Plum blossoms far and near:
My routine these days
Is strolling under them.

Someone may live
Beyond the plum bush:
Shimmering light.

Plum flower temple:
Voices rise
From the foothills.

Painting of plums by Sōseki.

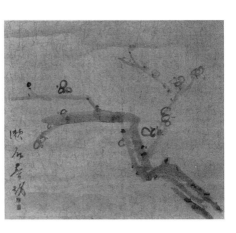

Nodding with drowsiness
On horseback:
Journey in spring.

The bottom of the tub
Drying on the hedge:
Spring sunshine.

Wish I could be
Reborn as small a man
As a violet.

Draped with haze,
The vermilion-lacquered bridge
Disappears.

My one hand these days,
Not clapping but clutching
A flounder at ebb tide.

To imagine the "sound of one hand clapping"
is one of the most famous koans of Zen.

A rutting cat
Has grown so thin:
Almost nothing but eyes.

East winds blowing,
Cloud shadows wrapping
The entire mountain.

A sparrow on a plum twig:
Silhouette of the blossoms on
The sliding paper screen—shaking.

The spring winds must show
Why Bodhidharma
Visited China.

"What is Bodhidharma's intention in coming east
to China?" is a set phrase asking "What is it that is
sought?" and by extension, "What is satori?"

In its fall
Trapping a worm:
A camellia blossom.

Up the hill of pine trees,
Rushing to worship:
Sunrise on New Year's Day.

Falling
Down into the heavens:
A skylark.

Painting of pine by Sōseki.

Bamboo woven
Into a fence:
A spring hut.

Bodhidharma kite
Hissing against the wind
With dignity.

Toward a Zen monk
The flag flapping:
Spring wind—

From a koan in *The Gateless Gate*. Observing a flag flapping in the breeze, one monk opined that the flag itself was moving, while another monk believed it was the wind that moved. The Sixth Patriarch concludes: "It's neither the wind nor the flag; it is your mind that moves."

After the butterfly's gone
It settles down:
A kitten.

The moon is up:
Plum blossom shadows
Fall on my pillow.

Somewhere
Someone calls my name:
A spring mountain.

Crazy butterfly
Flirting with flowers
Honoring the dead.

An inch of weight
On the nandina:
Spring snow.

Painting of bamboo by Sōseki.

33

Dry grass burning over
This hill and that field:
Pheasants' cries.

New Year's dream:
Not about finding money
Or about death.

A flower shadow
Creeps and overlaps
A beauty's.

Warbler eating flowers:
Are its droppings also
Red?

Spring rain:
Lying flat on the mat to see
The plum trunk level.

Spring rain:
Clinging to each other
Under one umbrella.

Spring rain:
Come inside my nightgown,
You nightingale, too.

Painting of two Zen monks by Sōseki.

Spring creek
Flowing,
Embracing the rock.

Huge Mount Fuji, reflected
On the balls of my eyes:
Spring pavilion.

You rude plum,
Suddenly appearing before me
On the cliff corner.

Fluttering in twos,
Next moment as one:
Butterflies.

No rain, it seems,
Yet the flowers
Are cloaked in dew.

Without a word
A white plum tree's
Blossomed.

A Zen motto goes: Teaching beyond teaching /
No leaning on words and letters. / Point straight at
a man's mind; / See its nature and become Buddha.

Gone with the bells
A hundred and eight illusions:
New Year's morning.

Bubbling,
Seeping through the sand:
Spring water.

Over the magnolia,
Dreamy
Drizzle falling.

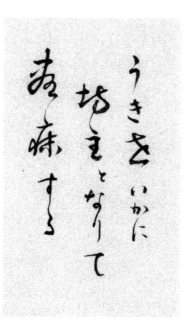

Letting the world be:
I'm a monk, having an
Afternoon nap.

夏 *Summer*

To Tsuchiya Chūji
August 27, 1898

Zen is not words or phrases but actual prac-
tice, isn't it? If you are in the dusty world
and buffeted at the mercy of it, then I won-
der if there's any difference between the
Zen life and the Zenless life . . .

To Zen monk Kimura Genjō
August 25, 1914

I am happy to know that your health is getting better and I hope you will soon visit Kobe again for Zen practice. As for me, everything is as usual . . . Are you lying in bed in the midst of this heat? According to Zen teaching, lying in bed is also Zen, isn't it? Sometimes I become absent minded, so I take an afternoon nap—this seems good for my brains . . .

A red sun
Falls into the sea:
What summer heat!

Letting the world be:
I'm a monk, having an
Afternoon nap.

Sticky hot!
Cicada sounds join my
Afternoon-nap dream.

The dog goes away—
Pop
Up again: daffodils.

Wrapped within
Young leaves:
The sound of water.

Horseflies,
Oxflies, all welcome:
Country inn.

The sea is near; a long
Walk, however, within this
Yellow-flower field.

Oops! Umph!
Got it! Killed a fly:
Houseboy's room.

Tim-id-ly
Sitting on the banana leaf:
A rain frog.

Biting at mosquitoes,
Nothing but mouth:
A toad.

The moment struck,
It expels a noon mosquito:
A wooden drum.

Now gathering,
Now scattering,
Fireflies over the river.

A wooden drum (mokugyo).

Watch birth and death:
The lotus has already
Opened its flower.

How cool is the shadow
Of green pine needles
On my napping face!

Buzzes encircle
A monk in samadhi:
Mosquitoes.

Samadhi, from the Sanskrit, is a Buddhist term for
physical and mental concentration.

Pebbles on the riverbed
Wavering:
Clear water.

Peaks of cloud:
The ship has crossed
A windless sea.

Opening alone,
Fragrant in the sun:
A hollyhock.

A snail
Raising its horns:
Edge of the well.

My dead mother
Frequents my mind:
Wardrobe-changing season.

Hollyhocks, flowers of summer.

So much weight
Lost to summer heat—
Even mosquitoes won't nibble.

Weight-lost,
Sun-burnt,
What has become of the monks?

Into the field of
Yellow flowers,
The red setting sun!

Flea, you shall never escape.
But where have you gone?
A cuckoo's cry.

The flea escaped me, leaving
A blood-stained blanket:
Object of spite.

The muddy water,
A school of children
Swimming.

It's too deep
To go across, besides
I can't swim.

The sunset:
From the seabed
Heat rises.

The lamp once out:
Cool stars enter
The window frame.

One firefly
Flitting
Through the room.

Blasphemy!
Backside against the altar:
Fanning and cooling himself.

Firefly hunting
Has led me
To fall in the creek.

Enjoying the cool bush shade,
And bitten by
Mosquitoes.

Fan used by Zen priests.

和敬
清寂

Well, it's time
To go to bed, but—
That summer moon.

Short night's dream:
No time even to remember
The one I've had.

Through lush leaves,
Only a palm-sized view
Of the mountain temple.

Everyone, including me
Clad all in white, enjoying
The evening cool.

A cuckoo's cry—
Hard to get out:
In the midst of shitting.

This haiku was penned on the edge of a reply letter to an
invitation to a party (the "cuckoo's cry") by Prime
Minister Saionji Kimmochi, at a time when Sôseki was
busy with personal matters.

To Matsune Toyojirō
August 20, 1907

Someone asked: "What is the truth when a man and woman fall in love?" Sōseki answered, rolling his pen on the desk: "Gone to the West, gone to India."

A poem goes:

Spring creek
Flowing,
Embracing the rock.

Someone asked: "What is the truth when a woman leaves the man she has loved?" Placing his pen upright on the desk and pausing, Sōseki answered: "Every day is a good day."

A poem goes:

Blossoms fallen
Have blown away in
Crushed shadows.

In this letter Sōseki is playing the Zen master, enaging in Zen dialogues (*Zen mondō*) with an imaginary someone, and then capping them with his own verses. His responses are well-known set phrases of Zen.

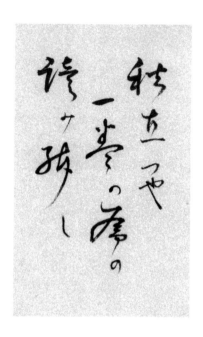

Autumn's already started:
There remains a book
Not yet read through.

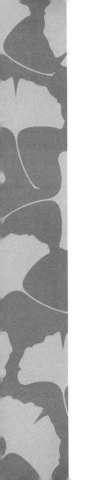

秋 *Autumn*

My house is not very good, but I think we can arrange lodging for you. Or you may try to stay at Saishō-ji if you prefer. It's a good temple and would be more comfortable than staying in our house. However, it may not be wise of you to limit yourself only to your usual temple life without experiencing this secular life of ours . . .

The two young Zen students visited our house wearing monks' robes and wooden clogs. Our children giggled at their clean-shaven, round heads. The visitors were quite good-natured and open-minded, not a bit nervous or irritable, but perhaps a bit absent-minded—in other words, dignified-looking and quite different from, frankly speaking, quite opposite from those young novelists or novelists-to-be who frequent my husband's study . . .

We had our lunch at a Western-style restaurant and one of the monks happened to drop half his steak on the floor under the table. The next moment, however, he coolly picked it up and ate it without hesitation. Before each meal they always put their palms together and bowed in prayer.

They ate everything without complaint and really ate like horses. My husband was very impressed with their frank and unpretentious attitude mixed with good manners and gratitude . . .

My husband was very curious about their stories of actual Zen monastery life, and he enjoyed one such innocent story: after the seven-day intense practice during the first week of December [*rōhatsu sesshin*], sweet sake is usually served, but with a limit of one cup per student, so everyone rushes to find as big a bowl as possible . . .

One of the two young monks grumbled, "I have to wash my clothes all by myself; no one will help me." The other instantly retorted, "It's only natural that everyone should hesitate, the way you pile up your dirty underwear!" All of these stories made my husband laugh but also feel some respect for the monks.

Their primitive Zen life, in fact, must have reminded my husband of his more typical acquaintances. All the people surrounding him were talented and socially adept . . . My husband constantly had to deal with such people, but their lives never engendered in him feelings of veneration. Besides, most of his acquaintances were, excitable, irritable, and argumentative, so often very difficult to deal with. He must have closely compared these people with the two simple Zen monks . . .

To Zen monk Kimura Genjō
November 10, 1916

Considering what little I could do for you during your stay here, I don't think I deserve such a polite letter of thanks . . . I admire the everyday attitude of Zen monks toward truth, and earnestly hope that you keep your presently fixed determination. As for me, I have decided to continue my self-seeking Zen practice in my own way and according to my capacity.

Examining my daily life, I find it very poor. Everything that I do—walking, standing, sitting, lying—is basically full of falsehood. I'm ashamed of it. When I next see you, I wish to make a better man of myself. You are twenty-two years old and I am fifty; thus I am twenty-eight years older, but with regard to *samadhi* insight and power, you are definitely more advanced.

High autumn sky:
Wish I could ride
The white cloud.

Autumn's already started:
There remains a book
Not yet read through.

Going autumn: sunlight
Peeks through the rafters
Slantways.

Bay in autumn:
The sounds of a stake
Driven into the ground.

Autumn fly:
I caught one
And let it fly.

Autumn mountains:
A dot of cloud
Calmly passed over.

Clear autumn sky
One pine tree
Soaring on the ridge.

Autumn winds—
Haunches of a cow on its
Way to be butchered.

In a letter to Matsune Tōyōjō (Toyojirō) of October 8,
1912, Sôseki relates that he composed this poem when
he went for a hemorrhoid operation.

Persimmon leaves:
On each,
Moonlight.

Morning glory:
A beauty's charm
But a few day's dream.

Painting of persimmon and bamboo by Sōseki.

Morning chill,
Evening chill,
Human warmth.

Morning chill,
Evening chill,
Alone I travel.

My renewed life:
How ancient
Autumn is!

Again I'm alive!
The height of the sky,
A red dragonfly.

One mountain shows
Various autumn
Colors of the bamboos.

To the end of the field
All alone I go:
Autumn sky.

腸に集ひて人をつのしや志きを恨
飛ぶもまた鳥も雅らうも照

漱石

Coming onto my shoulder,
Are you seeking a friend?
Red dragonfly.

Throw please, everyone,
All the chrysanthemums
Into the coffin!

"Coming onto my shoulder…"
calligraphy by Sōseki.

Lightning flash—
Each time the waterfall
Reveals its riverbed.

Under the leaves
Of a morning glory:
Cat's eyes.

My life recovered.
How happy I am!
Autumn in chrysanthemums.

Fog clears away:
The waterfall shows up
Bit by bit.

Dots of cloud coming,
Going over the waterfall:
Red maple leaves.

A cricket
Suddenly started singing,
Suddenly stopped again.

It's autumn, crickets,
Whether you may
Chirp or not.

White chrysanthemums:
My scissors for a while
Stop their motion.

No sake,
No poem,
Silence of the moon!

Small amount of sake
Remains in the bottle:
Chill of the night.

A dragonfly
Hovering by the stake
Two inches away.

Sheer cliff:
Not a single creeping ivy
To turn red.

One huge rock
On the riverbed:
Autumn water.

Zen temple:
No rain of sorrow
Falls on the banana leaves.

A verse from *A Zen Forest* goes:
Rain of no sorrow / falls / on banana leaves: / A man, /
hearing its pattering / feels his bowels cut.

In the chill
Each stone saint sits
In its own way.

Sunny place—
Feeling
Of a ripe persimmon.

"Sunny place . . ."
calligraphy by Sōseki.

夕あかりや熟柿のおちて

漱人

Shining in the wind
Of the new autumn:
A spider's thread.

Don't forget, sweet persimmon,
Your younger days when
You were still bitter.

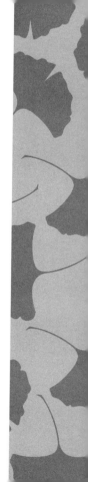

You, a Zen priest
Looking like a
Scarecrow.

Again to see things
In the original up and down:
The autumn mountain is new.

A five-tiered waterfall:
A maple color
On each tier.

The whole turns
Yellow:
Mandarin orange orchard.

Walking under the moon,
Sôseki has forgotten
All about his wife.

Breathing pauses in the
Monk's chant for the dead:
Grasshopper's chirp.

My life saved
By a hairbreadth:
Slender pampas stalk.

Was it a banana leaf
That surprised me with
Sudden knocks on the door?

Moonlit night:
Each silhouette
Moving.

All waving in the wind—
Tall and short—
Pampas flowers.

Nice to return
To my native town:
Chrysanthemum season.

To Buddha:
Best to dedicate
White chrysanthemums.

The Blue Cliff Record,
Theme of the sermon;
Temple night is long.

The *Blue Cliff Record*, a collection of one hundred
koans, verses, and commentaries completed in twelfth-
century China, is much used in the Rinzai sect of Zen.

Crowd of pampas grasses
Waving—
Beginning of autumn.

Coolness!
Sounds of the water after
All gone to bed.

Buddha Nature, if compared,
Must be this
White bell-flower.

In the millet field
All alone I'm harvesting:
Evening glow.

The morning sun
Pops up on
A thousand-mile millet field.

After harvesting
The surrounding millet,
Chrysanthemums left alone.

Just before me
The Spirit's moving:
Tip of my pen.

Near and far,
Everything's under the moon:
Seas and mountains.

Full moon:
Round is the shadow
Of a priest's head.

Tickling the
Skinny horse's haunches:
Autumn flies.

In the bush shade
No fish moves:
Autumn water.

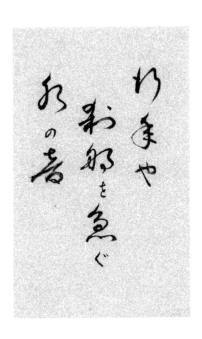

This passing year:
Sound of rushing water
Every moment.

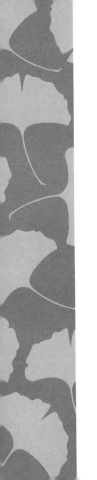

冬 Winter

To Saitō Agu
January 10, 1895

Since last December I have been staying in Kigen-in temple in Kamakura for personal discourse [*sanzen*] with Shaku Sōen Rōshi. For about ten days I maintained my "rice-bag" body with simple rice gruel in a broken-legged bowl in the Zen monastery. The day before yesterday, I climbed down from the temple and returned to Tokyo. Mercy on me who has failed to encounter my original self out of the five hundred lives of a fox in *samsara* . . .

Gate of the Kigen-in temple
of the Engakuji complex.

Now, I'll
Dare enter this tiger's cave:
This morning of a heavy snowfall.

Bowing a greeting:
From the woman's hair
A hailstone falls.

Family and world left behind,
No-minded myself: nevertheless
This severe blizzard!

People in the city
All busy with their own jobs:
End of the year.

Bowing and hugging
My knees—
Oh, the cold!

My robe dried
Both front and back:
Fire of firewood.

From this lukewarm hot-spring,
Hard to get out:
Brr!

Stepping on a wet
Washcloth in dead darkness:
How cold!

Emptiness, no holiness,
Bodhidharma's statue:
Daffodils in the water.

The *Blue Cliff Record* relates that Emperor Wu of Liang
asked Bodhidharma, "What is the first principle of the
holy truths?" The reply came, "Emptiness, no holiness."

Your talk began with a
Fart—
Well, well!

A crow takes off, leaving
The winter tree shaking
In the evening sun.

Drizzling:
A muddy cat asleep on
The holy sutra.

My hut:
Even the icicles
Greet a new year.

The old tablets:
Sweet-potato vines
Cover the temple gate.

Standing naked
In the winter wind:
Statues of the guardian gods.

Bitter winter wind:
No leaves left
To fall.

Winter wind echoes:
Following crookedly
The crooked path.

In the winter wind
The mountain peak
Soars like a sword.

Scent of daffodils
By the pillow of
A person with a cold.

Monk in samadhi
Still alive!
A winter moon.

The pack horse's back
Loaded with charcoal:
Spotted snow.

Must be cold:
The temple in the bamboo grove
To which the monks return.

Priest and layman
Sit by the hearth
Face to face.

Year after year
Sharpened by winter wind:
That mountain.

Passing year:
Our cat squats
Down in my lap.

Painting of two monks and calligraphy by Sōseki.

Sweeping it off, again
Sweeping it off, still
Snow on my sleeves.

Early winter:
The road to enlightenment,
Its gate closed yet.

A saying from *A Zen Forest* states: "One way to satori:
A thousand saints can't point it out."

One house is
Buried
Silent in the snow.

The winter wind has
Blown the evening sun
Into the sea.

Waiting for spring:
Indeed nothing happens
To a noble person.

A saying from *A Zen Forest* states: "To a man of satori,
nothing happens."

The radish dish:
Two shadows of
The round shaved heads.

Good or evil?
Eat the radish dish
And you'll know.

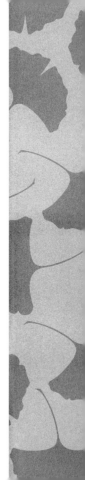

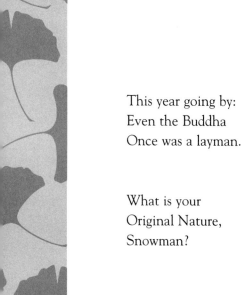

This year going by:
Even the Buddha
Once was a layman.

What is your
Original Nature,
Snowman?

The koan "What is your true original nature before your
father and mother are born?" was given to Sōseki by his
master, Shaku Sōen Rōshi.

Main hall of the temple:
Coldness
Of one hundred feet.

Confined within doors
A priest is warming himself
Burning a Buddha statue.

"Main hall of the temple . . ."
calligraphy by Sōseki.

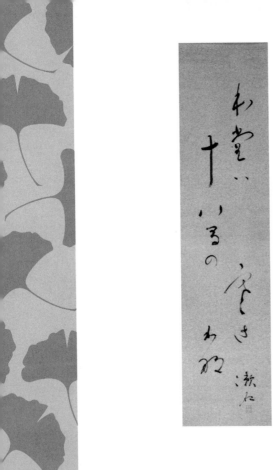

Against my eyes,
Mouth and everywhere:
Blizzard—

Sideways
Across the Musashino Plain:
Winter rain.

Autumn maple leaf
Falls
Rustling.

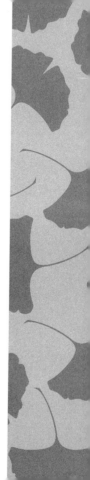

Country life:
Enough with some
Bushels of millet.

This passing year:
Sound of rushing water
Every moment.

While watching the Buddha
Even I remain
Buddha-minded.

I've left the world behind:
Even the busy streets
An ancient scene.

Not knowing why,
I feel attached to this world
Where we come only to die.

FROM A TALK BY D.T. SUZUKI
GIVEN AFTER SŌSEKI'S DEATH

A ten-day practice was not enough for Mr.
Natsume to achieve satori. It was true,
however, that he was very much gifted
with the spirit of Zen.

From a talk by Sōen Shaku

I don't know very much about Sōseki, but
I felt he was man gifted with a natural Zen
spirit. His Zen study was nothing much,
but he seemed to have touched the root
of Buddhism and Oriental philosophy.
"Following heaven, leaving self" is thought
to have been his motto during the last days
of his life, and this is obviously the very
point of Mahayana Buddhism.

Funeral poem by Sōen Shaku

Once he declined
   the fame
     of a doctorate,
Preserving humility,
   enjoying Zen spirit
     in layman's garb.
Right now he's gone
   the moment
     the pleasure ceased;
There remains a chilly lantern
   and the sounds
     of night rain.

Inklings Editions are a production of Weatherhill, Inc., publishers of fine books on Asia and the Pacific. Editorial supervision: Ray Furse. Book and cover design: Mariana Canelo Francis and D.S. Noble. Production supervision: Bill Rose. Printing and binding: Daamen Printing, West Rutland, Vermont.